Loving-Kindness

A Tiny Meditation Guide for All Beginners

Catherine Mie Ishida

Illustrations by Sophie Northcott

tti

Copyright © 2020 by Catherine Mie Ishida

All rights reserved. Your support of authors' rights are appreciated. Please contact the publisher for permission requests.

This Too Is
Hilo, Hawai'i
thistoois.com

Available anywhere books are sold. Support your local bookstore by ordering through them. Purchases of the paperback and ebook editions support the author. Purchases of the full color hardback edition support the illustrator.

Title: Loving-Kindness
Subtitle: A Tiny Meditation Guide for All Beginners
Author: Catherine Mie Ishida
Illustrator: Sophie Northcott
Publication Date: December 15, 2020 (Paperback First Edition)
Paperback ISBN: 978-1-7360952-0-1
E-Book ISBN: 978-1-7360952-2-5
Full Color Hardcover ISBN: 978-1-7360952-1-8

For all the bold, beautiful, and brainy people who sometimes need a bit of permission to be who we are.

Contents

Introduction 8
What is meditation? 10
Why start with loving-kindness? 14
What is loving-kindness? 18
What is loving-kindness practice? 22
How do I practice loving-kindness? 26
What is the right meditation posture for me? 32
Aside: Stillness 36
Why safety, health, happiness, and ease in this world? 38
Aside: Self-Check 42
How do I choose whom to name in my practice? . 44
Aside: Fall in love! 52
How long should I practice? 54
What if I only have a minute? 58
What if I don't even have a minute? 60
Aside: Belly-Breaths 66
When should I practice? 68
Where should I practice? 72
Can I change the wording? 76
Can I change the sequence? 80

Is practicing alone enough? 84

What next? 86

Epilogue: How My Life Has Changed Since Starting the Practice 92

Thank You! 94

About the Author 97

About the Illustrator 99

Introduction

In January 2020, I chose to experiment with loving-kindness meditation for the year. It's a simple practice: in a calm state, slowly, gently, and deliberately wish for safety, health, happiness, and ease in this world for yourself, a beloved person, a neutral person, a challenging person, and all beings.

Little did I know that in a matter of weeks, the whole world would be wishing each other safety and health!

This tiny guide is an invitation for you to join me in this beautiful and profound practice. It's a collection of tips and insights that might inspire you to try this practice for yourself.

What if we lived in a world where people always, truly, and sincerely wish for the safety, health, happiness, and ease for themselves and others, no exceptions?

What if we lived in a world where everyone knows how to love and to be kind?

What if we lived in a world where we all know how to begin again quickly and compassionately every time we experience a stumble, fall, road block, setback, disappointment, or betrayal?

What if we lived in a world where everyone felt deeply loved? Sustained by loving-kindness?

These hopes are my stars, and stars can guide, even when beyond reach.

What is meditation?

What does the word "meditation" bring to your mind?

The word "meditation" came into the English language through the Latin word "meditatio," which means "the act of thinking or planning."[1] Casually, someone might say "let me meditate on that" to mean "let me think about that."

More strictly, the word distinguishes ordinary thinking from intentionally focusing one's attention on a topic or object and noticing the thoughts and feelings that arise. If a person then puts those thoughts and feelings into written form, those words are also called "a meditation."[2]

For example, in Shakespeare's play, Hamlet picks up the skull of the court jester Yoric, and meditates on death. Death and Shakespeare's words are perennial favorites for contemplation, a close synonym for "meditation" when used in this sense.

---

[1] https://en.wiktionary.org/wiki/meditation and https://en.wiktionary.org/wiki/meditatio#Latin

[2] https://www.merriam-webster.com/dictionary/meditation

Based on this traditional meaning, this tiny guide could be called a meditation. It's a summary of my thoughts on loving-kindness practice written in the hope that it might guide you in your contemplation on life.

However, since the late 20th century, the word meditation has taken on meanings that encompass a wider variety of contemplative practices from a wide variety of cultures, often South Asian. When I do an internet search on the word "meditation," I find images similar to the cover illustration of this book: someone sitting crossed-legged surrounded by colorful clouds! It took intentional digging to find an image of the painting "The Philosopher in Meditation," often attributed to Rembrandt.[3] There are similarities between these 17th century and 21st century scenes: a person sitting, bathed in light. But the differences are just as striking: what is dark, who is sitting, outdoor versus indoor setting, and the presence or absence of a book.

For this tiny guide, I would like to adopt a simple definition that aligns with the contemporary usage of the word without introducing too many

---

[3] https://en.wikipedia.org/wiki/Philosopher_in_Meditation

assumptions about how it might be done. Here is one from *Psychology Today*:

> Meditation is a mental exercise that trains attention and awareness.[4]

Athletes train to bring out their full capacity as an athlete. Everyone can train to bring out our full capacity as a conscious being.

---

[4]https://www.psychologytoday.com/us/basics/meditation

Why start with loving-kindness?

Would you like to...

- Meditate for the first time?
- Try a new or different meditation practice?
- Accomplish a task that is meaningful yet challenging?
- Be a kinder, more loving you, more of the time?
- Live in a just, equitable, and sustainable world?
- Exercise free will?

If you answered yes to any of the questions above, a loving-kindness meditation practice may be for you.

Here are some reasons why I recommend loving-kindness meditation to all:

- Meditation is good for you. If you are not sure yet, give it a try or do a little research. (An internet search on "science meditation benefits" is a good start.)

- Loving-kindness practice builds upon something you probably already do regularly: wishing people well.
- Loving-kindness is an easy entry into meditation practice because it offers something specific and meaningful for your mind to do.
- Loving-kindness meditation is simple and self-guided. You can practice it anywhere in the Universe.
- Common side effects of loving-kindness meditation include calmness, like many other meditation practices, but also an immediate sense of gratitude and joy.
- Loving-kindness practice cultivates qualities known as the "four brahmavihārās" in Buddhism, loving-kindness, compassion, and joy-in-the-joy-of-others, and equanimity.
- Loving-kindness practice cultivates qualities knowns as "positive psychological capital," hope, self-efficacy, resilience, and optimism.
- Loving-kindness practice cultivates self-compassion. The practice itself helps the practitioner continue through frustrations and setbacks. This skill is transferable to any meaningful and challenging endeavor.

- Loving-kindness can interrupt patterns of trauma. One of the barriers to a just and equitable world is the immense trauma people have been passing on from generation to generation. People often re-enact trauma unknowingly, even when they are trying not to, and perhaps occasionally because they are trying so really, very, hard not to. Loving-kindness practice slows people down and creates opportunities to notice and evaluate habitual behaviors.
- When you guide yourself in loving-kindness practice, you have consented to the content. You know the script and the guide well. You are connecting with values that you have consciously chosen.
- With the human population around eight billion, it would take more than twelve hundred years of non-stop loving-kindness practice for one person to offer well-wishes to each person alive today. The more people there are practicing loving-kindness, the more loving-kindness there will be.

What is loving-kindness?

What is love?

What is kindness?

What is loving-kindness?

These questions are explorations for a lifetime, but there is a simple way to put these words and ideas into relationship:

> Loving-kindness is the state of being from which loving feelings and kind actions flow.

Combining the words "love" and "kindness" highlights how feelings, intentions, and actions are inseparable, and makes the claim that there is a "state of being" from which these arise spontaneously and with ease.

Strictly speaking, loving-kindness is the English translation of a concept central to Buddhist teachings. The word is "maitrī" in Sanskrit and "mettā" in Pali.

These words and many others in different languages are like snow that falls in different places, all snow, but soft and fluffy here, and crystalline and crunchy there. However, inside the DNA of the word loving-kindness is a particular insight nurtured by Buddhist communities:

> Cultivate the right state of being, and right action will follow.
>
> Cultivate loving-kindness, compassion, equanimity, and joy-in-the-joy-of-others, and right action will follow.

This is a book on loving-kindness practice so I won't address compassion, joy-in-the-joy-of-others, and equanimity directly, but they are inseparable from loving-kindness. Cultivate any one of these qualities, and the others will arise. As you practice, you may experience this yourself.

What is "right action" in any culture is complex and nuanced, but many have developed single-sentence reference guides. Here are some examples:[1]

---

[1] I found these among examples listed in the Wikipedia article on the "Golden Rule."

- One should never do something to others that one would regard as an injury to one's own self. In brief, this is dharma. Anything else is succumbing to desire. (From the Mahābhārata 13.114.8, Critical Edition)
- What is hateful to you, do not do to your fellow: this is the whole Torah; the rest is the explanation; go and learn. (Attributed to Hillel the Elder, Shabbath folio:31a, Babylonian Talmud)
- You shall love the Lord your God with all your heart, with all your soul, with all your strength, and with all your mind; and love your neighbor as yourself. ("The Great Commandment," attributed to Jesus of Nazareth, Luke 10:25 - 28)
- Zi gong (a disciple of Confucius) asked: "Is there any one word that could guide a person throughout life?" The Master replied: "How about '恕' (reciprocity) - never impose on others what you would not choose for yourself?" (The Analects XV.24)

These "rules" do not capture the fullness of each culture and their deep trove of stories, value systems, and practices. And yet, when forced to prioritize, ethical systems in various cultures arrive at similar understandings of what it means to be human, and how best to relate to one another: reciprocity and interdependency, relationship, equality, shared destiny...

Loving-kindness (along with compassion, joy-in-the-joy-of-others, and equanimity) is a state of being in which these rules describe your behaviors, not prescribe them.

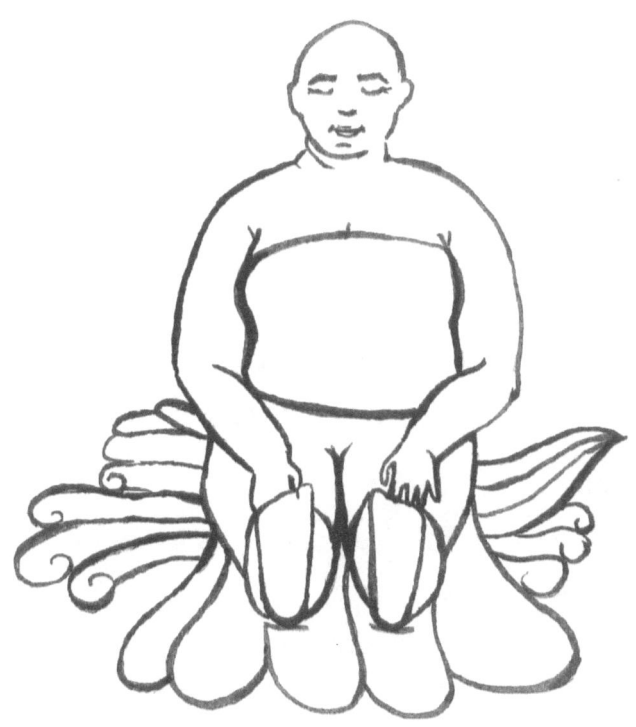

What is loving-kindness practice?

Loving-kindness practice is intentionally setting time aside to wish people well in a specific way.

There are many "specific ways" to do the practice, and the greatest variation among them is in the language people use for well-wishing. The version in this book follows meditation teacher Sharon Salzberg's[1] recommendation to wish people:

- Safety,
- Health,
- Happiness, and
- Ease.

Common to different variations of the practice are the general categories of people to wish well for:

- Yourself
- People who inspire good feelings and actions in you
- People who are neutral to you

---

[1] Visit her website www.sharonsalzberg.com or read her book *Lovingkindness: The Revolutionary Art of Happiness*.

- People who bring up negative feelings in you

And, the biggest difference between everyday well-wishing and loving-kindness practices is that loving-kindness practice requires two commitments:

- Setting an intention to extend your well wishes to all living beings, without exception.
- Expanding your sense-of-self to encompass the whole Universe.

If you are unready or unwilling to make these commitments, then loving-kindness practice is not for you at this time.

You may of course wish people well in many ways and generate loving feelings and do kind acts, and you will be doing good for the world and for yourself. It just won't be loving-kindness practice as most practitioners understand it, and you shouldn't expect to experience the full benefits of the practice.

There are two main reasons not to permit ourselves any exceptions:

- Allowing any exception starts us down a slippery slope of trying to determine who is and who isn't deserving of loving-kindness and why. Humanity has a dismal record latching onto judgements and justifying cruelty. Everyone is potentially unworthy of love and kindness if any one of us is. Many of us know this deeply in our bodies, whether we are aware of it or not. Many of us have a part of us that always feels unsafe.

- Allowing no exceptions affirms the possibility of healing for all people. There are abusive, cruel, evil, narcissistic, unthoughtful, negligent, misguided people in the world. These are broken people. It is OK to wish that they heal, so they cause no more harm. If all of us are deserving of love and kindness, then each and every one of us is. Many of us have a part of us that isn't sure if this is true.

Loving-kindness practice is a gentle reminder that none of us deserve to suffer from abusive, cruel, evil, narcissistic, unthoughtful, negligent, misguided behavior.

We should hold people accountable for their actions. And we should hold them in loving-kindness at the same time. This is how we interrupt cycles of harm.

How do I practice loving-kindness?

This version builds on the well-wishes that people spontaneously offer each other in times of crisis. It's what has "stuck" to me, and I share it with the hope that it may be sticky for you. It's a variation on Sharon Salzberg's interpretation of the practice.[1]

1. Settle into your space. Ideally, you are somewhere you won't be interrupted, and can make yourself physically comfortable for however long you choose to practice. Pick a posture. What works for you to be relaxed and alert at the same time? What would minimize strain and pain in both the short and long term? Seated postures with your spine aligned and supported from your hips to the top of your head work well. Any number of reclined postures with your spine supported work well too. Use cushions and other props to make sure the rest of your body isn't straining. Gather any objects that you would like near you to mark this time as special.

---

[1]Sharon Salzberg's current teaching uses the phrase "live with ease" instead of "be at ease in this world."

2. Settle into your body. If it makes you comfortable, take a few deep breaths. Notice how you are in your body today. Feel how you are supported. Connect with the reasons why you chose to practice.
3. Begin. If you like, ring a bell, light a candle, bow, clap your hands, or take another deep breath to announce "you are beginning."
4. **Offer well-wishes to yourself.**

Invite the following phrases into your mind:

> May I be safe.
>
> May I be healthy.
>
> May I be happy.
>
> May I be at ease in this world.

Find a slow and soothing rhythm and repeat the set of phrases several times. Repeating the phrases three to seven times is a good place to start. Don't worry if the order gets mixed up. This happens. Begin again with any phrase.

5. **Offer well-wishes to those for whom well-wishes flow easily and earnestly.**

Bring to mind the people you are really truly grateful to have in your life. They may be the people who fill you with warm fuzzy feelings (at least most of the time) or they may not. They can be human or another type of animal. Choose one of them, a living being, and wish them well:

(In the following phrases, substitute "THEY" with the name, description, or pronoun of the person or being.)

>   May THEY be safe.
>
>   May THEY be healthy.
>
>   May THEY be happy.
>
>   May THEY be at ease in this world.

Linger here, repeating your well-wishes for this person. If the time you've set aside for practice allows, offer well-wishes to others as well, gradually extending your circle of care from those whose presence in your life you are intensely grateful for to those whose presence in your life you simply enjoy.

Start with spending at least half of your time in the first two parts.

6. **Offer well-wishes to those for whom your feelings are neutral.**

These are probably most of the people in your life: people you know but not well enough to have a strong feeling about one way or the other. These are the people to whom you're willing to offer an opening gesture of good-will.

> May THEY be safe.
>
> May THEY be healthy.
>
> May THEY be happy.
>
> May THEY be at ease in this world.

Take your time to explore the possibilities of whom to name here. Think of all the tiny interactions that dot your day, and the people you haven't met but make your life possible.

7. **Offer well-wishes to those who challenge you.**

These are the people towards whom your good-will won't flow without effort, and people with whom you have an adversarial relationship. Start with the easier cases, such as people who may have annoyed you briefly. Perhaps the person who suddenly pulled out in front of you while you were on the road, for example.

May THEY be safe.

May THEY be healthy.

May THEY be happy.

May THEY be at ease in this world.

One person in this category is enough for each practice session.

When you feel ready, offer well-wishes to others who have knowingly or unknowingly harmed you or your beloveds. Wish for them the safety, heath, happiness, and ease in this world so that they can stop harming.

8. **Extend your well-wishes to all beings, throughout our Universe, and extend your sense-of-self to all of existence.**

"Extending your sense-of-self" may feel tricky at first. Horse riders often describe feeling "at-one" with their horse while riding. An airplane pilot may feel like they ARE the plane. Imagine your skin gradually expanding beyond your body, your neighborhood, the planet and beyond. Or imagine you have an invisible arm reaching for the horizon. Once you find a way to feel a little larger than usual, fill yourself with well-wishes for all.

May all beings be safe, healthy, happy, and at ease in this world.

Rest in this state of being for as long as you like.

9. End. When you are ready or the time you set aside for practice is up, deliberately end your practice. Repeat or reverse the actions you took to begin your practice: ring a bell, blow out your candle, bow, clap your hands, or take another deep breath.

10. Check-in briefly with yourself. You've been physically still for a while. Do you need to stretch? Did something come up during your practice that you want to follow up with later? Take a note of it.

11. Return your space and stuff to their "home" state. They may not be alive, but they too can be held in loving-kindness.

What is the right meditation posture for me?

There are likely to be several. Experiment, find what's comfortable for you, and if you can, seek out the advice of an expert on body posture early on. Physical therapists, experienced yoga teachers, chiropractors, and Aston patterning practitioners are all possibilities.

All bodies are different and all bodies are adaptable, for better or worse.

Do you know any tall people who seem to have a permanent slouch? Being singled out as being "so tall" over and over again can weigh a person down.

Or...

Driving a car everyday may mean that you use your right leg more than your left leg, and your right pelvis starts to get stuck in a forward tilt, which changes the effective length of your legs, which means you walk slightly lopsided, which yanks the muscles on one side of your back which pulls the shoulder on the opposite side so you have a slight headache every day but nothing you can't put up with.

Or...

Half your body is paralyzed from a stroke. You've trained the other half of your body to be strong enough to take care of all of you.

In meditation, your ideal postures will allow your body to be soft and stable at the same time. You want a stable foundation that can support your spine in as neutral a position as your body allows. Beyond the minimal effort to support your spine, you want your muscles to relax.

If your mind can stay alert as you relax, it's a good time to meditate. If you fall asleep, you probably need that sleep.

Having succeeded in adapting to various forms of stress, many of us struggle to remember what "soft and stable" feels like and to discover intuitively postures that will be safe and comfortable for both the short and long-term.

I don't drive much, but my pelvis has a tendency to twist itself. Most of the time I don't notice it at all. But more often than I'd like, as stress piles up, my back muscles give up, and I end up spending weeks on a sofa to recover.

Thankfully, a wonderful yoga teacher took a quick look at me (at a time when I was feeling just fine) and noticed a tilt in my pelvis and its impact on my standing posture. They recommended that I be careful about lingering in asymmetrical yoga poses, and suggested that I meditate in a kneeling position, which is symmetric from left to right.

My default meditation posture is now sitting straddled on a tall cushion. When I meditate with other people, I gaze over heads hovering several feet below my own. It's embarrassing, but at least I'm not courting weeks of pain. I still sit cross-legged sometimes, without actually crossing my legs, again on a tall cushion, switching legs frequently. I also mediate lying down with and without props.

Doing an internet search on "meditation postures" will give you many sitting, standing, and prone options to try, and your body may be able to accommodate some of them. You can also try various "relaxing yoga poses." Walking and other forms of movement that you can practice safely while withdrawing most of your attention from your external environment are good to have in the mix.

Once you find some poses that seem promising, ask someone to help you fine tune them. If you're not ready to ask an expert, ask a friend. Ask them to describe how you are supporting your spine, your hips, legs, and feet, your arms and hands, your neck and shoulders, your head, chin, ears, and the crown of your head, and your face, jaw, brow, and eyes. You can invite them to gently touch those parts of your body to give you tactile feedback as they offer their observations. They may suggest that you try a completely different pose all together. That is great information that you could choose to act on.

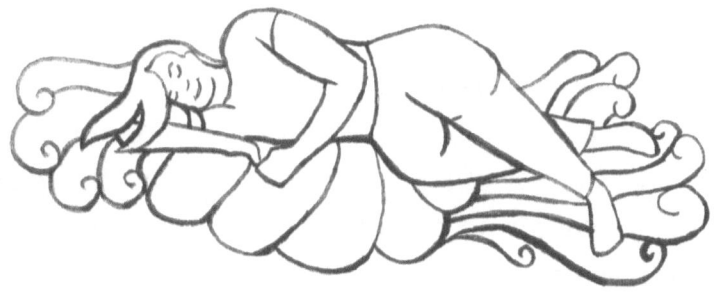

Aside: Stillness

Stillness of the body is helpful in meditation only to the extent that it supports stillness of the mind. There are many traditional forms of meditation that include small movements such as swaying, circling, and rocking, as well as those that include big movements such as twirling. Give yourself permission to move as you are so moved.

Stillness of the mind is hard to describe, and really only comes in degrees. If you've received any instructions to empty your mind, put them aside for the moment. Stillness of the mind is the ultimate goal of yoga[1], and it's as elusive as the Holy Grail in tales of King Arthur.

Imagine your mind as a stage crowded with and surrounded by young children. Some are clamoring to get into the spotlight, some of them are curled up in the shadows trying not to be noticed, and some seem to have no care about what is going on. You are the director of a play and the children are your cast. Your job is to take in the whole scene and invite the children into the spotlight one at a time.

---

[1]The second sentence in the Yoga Sutras by Patanjali states "Yogaścittavṛttinirodhaḥ," or "yoga is the cessation of the movement of the mind."

In loving-kindness meditation, you are inviting your well-wishes for all beings to be in the spotlight. When other thoughts appear, acknowledge them, "Hi Shopping List!" And then gently usher them out, "Not right now, Project Due Today. Wait for your turn, please."

I imagine stillness of the mind as the opposite of emptiness. As an openness to all sensations and thoughts, holding them in soft focus attention equally and lovingly. As an awareness of the mind as a stage, still in the midst of commotion.

Why safety, health, happiness, and ease in this world?

Safety, health, happiness, and ease in this world are basic human needs. They motivate us and shape what is possible for us.

Whether or not you have ever meditated before, you've probably thought about safety, heath, happiness, and ease in this world, and wished them for yourself and others. It's easier to imagine and practice something you've already experienced.

As concepts, they are a bit smaller in scope than love, justice, or "universal goodwill." A little more tangible, concrete, and familiar.

And yet, if they are to be achievable goals for any one of us, we may all need to reflect on their meaning throughout our lives.

One reason for revisiting their meaning is that safety, health, happiness, and ease in this world looks, feels, smells, sounds, and tastes differently to different people, and then changes with time and circumstance. When it comes down to specifics, there is no one size fits all. Even if we think we have a general sense of what safety, health, happiness, and ease in this world means, to know what that is for a particular person, we need to know something about their specific challenges, hopes, fears, and sources of joy.

Another reason is that many of us are deeply confused about our deepest most fundamental needs.

If anybody wants to influence our behavior in any way, if they are good at it, for better or for ill, they will appeal to our basic needs.

We continuously take in quiet and loud, explicit and implicit messages that say: "You feel unsafe, don't you? This is how you are unsafe, do this and you will be safer!," "You don't feel right, do you? Well, that's because something about you is wrong, and here's how to fix it.", "You want to be happy? You need this!," "You want to be free, free of pain, stress, limitations, suffering, constraints, illusions, don't you? Don't you? This is your path to salvation." Once these messages are inside us, it's hard to get them out. At least, it takes some skill (and practice of course!)

Interdependence

Individual well-being and collective well-being are inseparable.

People arrive at this awareness in different ways. You can get there through an examination of the natural world and the study of ecology. You can reach there through sacred stories that describe the unity of all creation. You can journey there by contemplating how life emerges from itty-bitty particles bound by the physical rules that govern our whole Universe. You can travel there from teachings on interdependence.

Let all the messages you receive on safety, health, happiness, and ease in this world pass through the sieve of interdependence. If you can reconcile a message with your awareness of the unity of individual and collective well-being, explore it for a while. If not trash it. Chances are the message will come your way again so you will have plenty of opportunities to re-examine it.

Do you wish for yourself and others "a beautiful home, a perfect family, and a great job?" Or do you wish for a safe home, a supportive family, and meaningful and satisfying work? A safe home may be beautiful, the people who surround and support you through times good and bad may be the perfect family for you, and meaningful and satisfying may be your definition of great. But why not go straight to the point and wish each other safety, health, happiness, and ease in this world?

Why not?

Aside: Self-Check

Sometimes we can get confused about what safety, health, happiness, and ease in this world mean, and how they feel.

Here are some questions to ponder now and then to check-in with reality rather than our fears.

What is safety?

- Are there people in your life who love and support you and affirm who you are as you truly are?
- Do you have access to a (mostly) stress-free environment every day?
- Are there places where there is no threat to your physical body, or hostility or discomfort with your presence or existence?
- Even for a short moment?

What is health?

- Do you have the capacity to experience loving-kindness, compassion, equanimity, and joy-in-the-joy-of-others?

What is happiness?

- Can you smile?
- Do you smile? Inwardly or outwardly?
- Do you find meaning in how you live?

What is ease in this world?

- Do you have the material, emotional, and spiritual support to sustain your safety, health, and happiness?
- Do you find joy and beauty in this world?
- Do you allow yourself to be nurtured by love and kindness when offered?
- Can you find calm in the midst of chaos?

How do I choose whom to name in my practice?

Focus on the Living

You want the people you name in your loving-kindness practice to meet these three criteria:

- They are physically alive!
- You know their actual name, how they look, or otherwise have some sense of who they are as an embodied real person.
- You are ready to name them.

The dead are not alive. Let us respect the very real threshold between the realm of the living and the realm of the dead, and maintain separate tool kits for tending to the dead and tending to the living. Reserve your loving-kindness practice for here and now in the realm of the living for which it was developed and where it is needed.

Loving-kindness practice is a mental rehearsal. How do you want to be the next time you encounter this person? The more vividly you can imagine them and make them "real," the better prepared you will be when you are in an actual situation where you want to benefit from your practice.

It's good to work though judgements we've developed or absorbed about people in certain roles and professions. Loving-kindness practice helps us do that by asking us to focus on the person, not their roles. You can name someone that you may never meet in person, but stay away from naming general roles or categories of people for the bulk of your practice. Name these at the very end of your practice, right before expanding your well-wishes to all of existence. You can, however, intentionally broaden your circle of care by choosing a particular role of category and finding someone to name from that role or category.

Loving-kindness practice asks that you name people who are challenging to you. Start with the easiest challenges. You can get to the really hard people, the ones that you really wished wouldn't cause you pain, when you are ready.

How do I know if I'm ready to name a challenging person?

Start by spending plenty of time naming yourself, the ones that fill you with a sense of immense gratitude, and the neutral people who make your days flow smoothly. Then name a person that challenges you. Maybe it's the store clerk that was slightly snippy when you asked them a question while they were busy restocking shelves. If your body stays relaxed and doesn't report back with a slew of upsetting feelings, then you can move on to name a person that is more challenging.

If you do get disturbed, pause, stop naming the person that triggered the disturbance, and take a moment to really feel what you feel.

If you know in your body that the pain of this relationship will overtake you, you are not ready. End your practice by offering well-wishes to yourself for a while and then releasing your well-wishes to the Universe.

However, you may find that alongside the pain there is a sense of spaciousness in you, that there is room in you to hold something more than just the uncomfortable sensations that this person has triggered in you. If so, imagine yourself in the biggest, warmest, loving embrace, and offer well-wishes to the other person at the same time. You may not be ready again tomorrow, or even days after that, but here and now, you are. Let this moment be, and then end your practice by releasing your well-wishes to the Universe.

Collect Beloveds

Beyond the three basic criteria, loving-kindness practice offers lots of flexibility for the practitioner. Eight billion people to choose from!

I recommend keeping lists, mental or physical, based on physical and emotional proximity. The goal is not to include everyone on your lists every time you practice. In any category, some people warrant being part of your practice every time, and some not.

Here are some categories to consider:

- Yourself!
- Deeply beloved people. These are the people who fill you with gratitude that they are part

of your life. Include at least one of them every time you practice. Let the happy hormones they trigger fill your body as you practice.

- People you spend a lot of time with. These may be friends, family, co-workers. The people for whom your practice is likely to have the largest immediate impact. These can include the most beloved and the most challenging people in your life. Include them all in your practice, as you are ready.

- People you will spend time with today. Prepare yourself to treat people with kindness.

- People with whom you have strong emotional bonds. These may be good but now far away friends, family, mentors, "enemies," "nemeses," "adversaries" and others with whom you've had some kind of power struggle. Maybe it's a person in the news that brings up "stuff" for you. If a person evokes strong feelings, positive or negative, they have a place in your practice.

- People you interact with regularly. They may be mail carriers, grocery stores clerks, bus conductors, or health care providers. These are the people that form the web of relationships that make our lives possible. "Regular" can indicate a range of frequencies. Once a day every day and once a year every year are both regular interactions.

- People you interact with occasionally. You may have a collection of business cards of people that you worked with in the past and thought you may want to call upon again if the opportunity arises. You may have a collection of old friends that you no longer keep up with.
- People to whom you are accountable. You may or may not be physically or emotionally close to these people, but you are responsible for their well-being in some way or another. Maybe these are customers, clients, members, contributors of a large business or organization that you are a part of. Maybe these are the people you serve as a public servant of some-kind.
- People who are accountable to you. These are the people whom we may or may not know personally whose decisions affect our lives.
- People who trigger you. These are the people you're not ready to include in your practice yet. One of the goals of loving-kindness practice is to be able to include them in the

future. Keep a list of these people so you can remember to move them to another list when you're ready.

Let People Go

One of the benefits of keeping lists is that you get to cull them. We are all responsible for the care for the web of all relationships, but we are not responsible for all of the care. Let the Universe, something-bigger-than-yourself, and other people do their part.

Consider removing from your lists:

- People who are no longer living.
- People with whom you interact rarely, if ever.
- People with whom you no longer have a relationship of accountability.
- People who have moved from the challenging to neutral category.

And ritualize your letting-go. You still wish these people well. They just won't be part of your loving-kindness practice anymore. Find other ways to honor the dead. Find a way to wish the living well and entrust their care to others. Take them off your lists.

If they're living, you can always add them back.

Aside: Fall in love!

Have you ever fallen in love?

Have you ever experienced a rush of dopamine, serotonin, oxytocin, and endorphins all at the same time?

Encountering a being who brings out the best in us is a true blessing.

However, these beings may not belong in your loving-kindness practice for various reasons:

- They may have never been alive.
- They may no longer be living.
- Your past or current reality with them may be dominated by other, more painful experiences.
- You may have just broken up with them.
- Your attachment to them may be unhealthy in some way.

Even so, cherish memories of being in love. It's ok to recall them before and while and after you practice. Keep your beloveds nearby, in body and in reminders.

If you haven't ever fallen in love, no worries. Loving-kindness practice can help those lovely hormones flow more easily through our bodies, and help us recognize true love when it comes our way.

How long should I practice?

As Long As You Can, Often

The short answer is: however long you can practice with a sense of ease, joy, and satisfaction, and however long you can practice without creating a sense of burden if you were to practice every day.

The Dalai Lama and Bishop Desmond Tutu, two respected spiritual leaders from two very different faith traditions, both spend about four hours every day in meditation/prayer.[1] Perhaps it takes that long for humans to explicitly name all the relationships that need our care and attention on any given day.

Perhaps someday all of us can be in meditation four hours a day with a sense of ease, joy, and satisfaction.

For now, what is "good enough" for most of us?

---

[1]From *The Book of Joy: Lasting Happiness in a Changing World* by the Dalai Lama, Desmond Tutu, and Douglas Carlton Adams.

I suggest starting with 10 minutes.

Ten minutes are long enough to:

- Go through a full practice of loving-kindness
- Make sure you will get distracted, and will have the opportunity to practice bringing your attention back to the moment
- Let your whole body settle
- Savor the sensation of loving-kindness when it arises

Ten minutes are short enough to:

- Fit into even the busiest of days
- Fit into several possible moments on a regular busy day
- Merge into your existing routines
- Allow you to disappear for a moment without triggering too much stress or hostile attention in others

If we can grant each other ten-minute bathroom breaks, we can grant each other ten-minute meditation breaks. There is a good chance that whatever is so important that there isn't ten minutes to spare in your day may actually be accomplished with greater ease and speed if you took the time to meditate.

Longer, Sometimes

And here is a longer answer: Meditation is a skill. Like any skill, the more we frequently and longer we practice, the more adept we get.

- Keep experimenting with what works for you. It may change over time.
- Longer is good!
- ...until it isn't.

Sometimes meditation practice can become a way to disengage from reality and other beings and avoid accountability. Sometimes meditation practice can become a harmful obsession. If so, you may not be able to judge that for yourself. Pay careful attention to the subtle and not so subtle feedback you are getting from others around you. If people around you seem more at ease, joyful, and satisfied around you, carry on. If not, reevaluate. Remember, some feedback you get will be more about the person giving the feedback, not you.

Meditate to strengthen the quality of relationships you have with those you care about. Ask a trusted person, a friend, teacher, counselor or coach, to help you reflect on the quality of your relationships, and evaluate whether the impact of your practice matches its intent. Adjust your practice accordingly.

Once you pick a length of time for a daily practice, give yourself enough time to form a new habit. Current research suggests that this can take 18 to 254 days.[2] If you are motivated by explicit goal setting, then choose a length of time to experiment with your choice of time and see if it "sticks." If not, no worries. Each day can be a new beginning.

- Short and frequent, is better than long and rare.
- Short and frequent plus long and rare is better than only short and frequent.

Let's agree that "frequent" means every day, and that "short," "long," and "rare" are for the practitioner to determine for themselves.

---

[2] An internet search on "how long does it take to form a habit?" will lead you to several articles that link back to research papers on the topic.

What if I only have a minute?

If I only have a minute, I

1. Pause
2. Let these words slowly fill my body:

    May each and every being be safe.

    May each and every being be healthy.

    May each and every being be happy.

    May each and every being be at ease in this world.

3. Pause
4. Let my mind and body relax until I choose to direct my attention somewhere else.

This is not a substitute for a longer everyday practice.

What I actually do is close my everyday practice with these words. If I only have a minute, I can invoke these words to remember the sensation of loving-kindness that is generated and stored in my body-memory through past practice.

For some people, loving-kindness is just a way of being that they've practiced their whole life. I need regular reminders, and it's good to have a way to access loving-kindness quickly.

What if I don't even have a minute?

Sometimes we want an instant reset button for stress. We can have several of these, and we can create them by incorporating our resets into our everyday practice.

Here are some of my instant resets that take only a single deep breath in and out:

In/Out

This is one of the classical forms of mindfulness meditation that trains the mind to pay attention to what is actually happening inside and outside us. As you breathe, say in your mind:

> I'm breathing in.
> I'm breathing out.
>
> In.
> Out.

Congratulations! You're breathing! You're alive, and have the capacity to know that you're alive!

Celebrate this small win, and carry on.

As you become accustomed to meditating, you can spend whole meditation sessions observing yourself breathing in and out. With practice, it's possible that you will find that just paying attention to your breath allows you to find calm and get into your "zone."

For some people, breathing deeply, or trying to breathe deeply, or being told to breathe deeply triggers anxiety. If that's you, don't force yourself to breathe deeply or meditate with phrases that include the word "breathe." Don't do anything that creates more stress! The practice isn't about breathing in any particular way. If you can do it with ease, just observe your breath as it happens naturally, noting the transitions between air entering your body and air going out with the words "in" and "out."

If focusing on your breath doesn't work for you, simply repeat a few words or a simple sound. The practices in this chapter link each in and out breath with a phrase or word, but you are free to set the breath aside and find a rhythm or even a melody that comforts you.

Relax/Smile

One of my favorite phrases to use in meditation comes from the teacher Thich Nhat Hanh and the communities of practice he inspired:

> Breathing in, I relax my body.
> Breathing out, I smile.
>
> (As you breathe in) Relax.
> (As you breathe out) Smile.

These words go straight to one of the main benefits of meditation: balancing the activity of the sympathetic and parasympathetic nervous system. For some reason I'm accustomed tensing with the in-breath and relaxing on the out-breath. Relaxing on the in-breath requires just enough focused attention and "do" energy, its seems funny that I am spending that on trying to relax and just "be." By the time I'm breathing out, I often have a genuine chuckle.

Repeating these words as you breathe in and out can be a whole meditation session. I recommend it as a practice of its own when you have time for many breaths and can infuse the words "relax" and "smile" with the power to help you relax and smile with a single breath.

Peace/Love (Or your choice!)

Breathing in, I breathe in peace,
Breathing out, I breathe out love.

Peace.
Love.

When I breathe in,
I breathe in peace,
When I breathe out,
I breathe out love.

With each and every breath,
May I breathe in peace.
With each and every breath,
May I breathe out love.

Each of these phrasings connects me to different communities of practice. The first and second phrasings are in the style of the Relax/Smile practice that comes to us through Thich Nhat Hanh. The third phrasing comes from a song by Sarah Dan Jones, a Unitarian Universalist musician and songwriter. In me, the harmonies of the song are inseparable from the words, and they echo in my body long after I've redirected my attention elsewhere. The last phrasing honors each distinct breath, reflecting how loving-kindness practice intentionally honors each distinct being. It reminds me not to get lost in the abstract.

I've chosen to close all my meditation practice sessions with these last two phrases. They are a genuine wish, and they give me a way home to loving-kindness when I only have time for a single breath to set my course.

I encourage you to find a phrase to close your meditation practice, whether you are practicing loving-kindness or some other form of meditation. Name the qualities and values you want to embody explicitly and often, so you can remember them when you need to.

Aside: Belly-Breaths

If alive, we all breathe, sometimes with help.

Remembering that we are breathing and feeling the rhythm of our breath can be comforting. No need to consciously alter our breath. Some of us can take deep breaths and feel more relaxed. Some of us can't and/or don't.

Take a moment to feel the gentle rise and fall of your belly away from and back towards your spine. Lying down makes focusing on this movement easier for most. If you can, place a hand on your belly and another on your heart or belly. Notice the sensations, thoughts and feelings that come and go or linger.

Just the sensation of your hand on your belly may be soothing.

If you want to experiment, imagine your whole torso is a balloon that expands with each in-breath, and lets air out with each out breath. Maybe the ballon is connected to a straw that sucks in air from your feet or your sits-bones. Take note of how your breathing changes and how it feels.

Hopefully, you are feeling more relaxed compared to when you started. When you're ready, let go of the balloon.

Whenever you need

- More air
- Your voice to be heard
- To sing
- To loosen the grip of something that feels suffocating
- To feel more alive

remember the sensation of breathing with your belly. Belly-breaths are also known as diaphragmatic breathing or eupnea, and it's how mammals breathe when we are relaxed.[1] We can't always force it, but if we can remember how it feels, we can help it show up.

---

[1] https://en.wikipedia.org/wiki/Diaphragmatic_breathing

When should I practice?

Great times to meditate are:

- Any time!
- Everyday
- On your Sabbath days, sometimes.

Every Day

Start with finding moments in your life where you can fit a ten minute or longer practice every day. For many people, this means before work, after work or during a longish work-break such as lunchtime.

Make an outline of your typical day, and for each hour, ask if there is a way to create ten minutes to pause and have a quiet moment for yourself. Each of those ten minute windows are yours to do something meaningful, not just meditation.

My favorite moments for meditation are right before work, and after I've restored order to the kitchen in the evening. Before work is my favorite.

It feels good to get a "to-do" completed early in the day, and tap into "I'm ready for life!" energy just as I need it. When I meditate in the evening, I make it the first relaxing activity at the end of the day. It's easier to relax even more when you are already relaxed! But often it also changes how I want to spend my remaining moments of wakefulness. It gives all the various parts of me to check-in with my command center and say: "Actually, THIS is how I would like to unwind right now."

Perhaps you already have a morning, evening, or even lunch-time routine. Let your meditation practice become a part of it.

Most of us have times in our daily schedule that are "squishy-er" than others. Perhaps you've made allowances for traffic delays, lingering in the shower, or just how long it might take to get dinner on the table. Are there times that are squishy and stretchy enough to include ten minutes when you don't have to do anything except stop, breathe, and rest in loving-kindness?

Once you have a list of possible moments, pick one, and see if it works. If not, try another time until you find your favorite.

For regular practice to be enjoyable and sustainable, you may need variety. Start with loving-kindness and then add other forms of meditation to your list of options for your daily practice.

Sabbath Days

Sabbath taking is the practice of intentionally taking time off from ALL "work" and enjoying the goodness in the world.

Once you've established a daily routine, review your calendar for the upcoming, weeks, months, and years. Schedule days to intentionally break your routine, and take a complete rest from all your ordinary tasks.

Everybody needs time off. Everybody needs to be able to imagine what it might feel like to have no stress or no externally imposed obligations for a day. This is a fundamental human need, and without it we cannot flourish. How can we know how much stress we are carrying, how much harm we are enduring, how distorted our awareness or reality might be, if we aren't able to calibrate our zero-point?

Please, practice Sabbath taking.

It's a reality that some of us can't take time off. If that is true for you, take note that you are being deprived of a fundamental human need. Know that a sincere desire for your safety, health, happiness, and ease in this world can only exist in the presence of a sincere desire that you have the time to be who you are.

Once you're able to practice Sabbath taking, there will be plenty of opportunities to enjoy longer meditation sessions if and when you want to.

Where should I practice?

For any kind of meditation practice, consider two goals:

1. Creating a habit
2. Bringing the benefits of your practice into the world

A Home for Your Practice

To make meditation practice a habit, you want to be able to quickly create an inviting physical space where you can:

- Establish a boundary of calm.
- Create a sense of sanctuary.

Having a specific place that you can return to on most days, a home for your practice, makes it easier to practice regularly. You may already know where you want to practice. If not, make a list of places where you might be able to establish boundaries of calm that could limit interruptions.

Physical distance, physical blocks, various sensory signs, and explicit agreements with people can all establish boundaries. Sitting cross-legged on a mountain top reachable only by clawing through thorny bushes on a remote island establishes a boundary. Letting people around you know that "When I am doing this, I'm meditating. Please don't disturb me. I promise to be with you within 10 minutes." can work too. There is usually a solution somewhere in-between these extremes.

Creating a sense of sanctuary is a bit more complex and personal. On a physical level, a sanctuary is a place where, once inside, your stress level drops. For each candidate home for your practice, imagine tweaks you might make to put yourself more at ease.

Some people prefer to minimize sensory stimuli. Silent meditation and meditating with closed eyes are common practices. In some Japanese traditions, practitioners face a blank wall with eyes gently open. Some people prefer the inclusion of carefully chosen stimuli. Tibetan traditions offer the option of gazing upon mandala of intricate and colorful patterns, for example.

If you are exposed to popular media, you probably have some expectations about what meditation looks, sounds, and feels like. It's ok to get inspiration from the broader world. You may also want to consider a subtler definition of sanctuary: a place where you feel open to receiving guidance from your most fundamental sources of value and meaning, and from your whole self.

A room with no windows may be the only place where you can establish a boundary of calm. If so, turning the lights off and closing your eyes may be all you need to do turn it into a home for meditation. Maybe you will need to bring an LED candle and a photo of a beloved person to turn the same room into your sanctuary.

Give some places a try and when you find a place that invites you back, make it your home for meditation.

Take Your Practice into the World

Once you have a home for your practice, you can go on adventures! Practice on a busy street corner, during a meeting, while you are vacuuming, in front of a grand view, with music. Keep notes of the conditions that support your practice and those that distract. Learn from experience. In time, you may find that you have the capacity to travel with a sanctuary within you.

Can I change the wording?

Thank you for asking! I hope you will experiment with the wording in this book for some time before you make changes.

I've encountered two ways people want to change the wording.

1) Changing "may my beloved be safe" to "I wish my beloved were safe."

Even if you disagree with delegating the work of making the world a better place to the supernatural or some unidentifiable force of nature, remember that you cannot make the world a better place by yourself.

The "may" language does two things. First, it declares our well-wishes in a way that is open to all the possible ways that our wishes may come true. Two, it gives our well-wishes a life of its own.

Leaving out the subject of who is doing the wishing and being ambiguous about how we might manifest our intention helps us by-pass whatever might be in us that resists offering loving-kindness to ourselves and others. This resistance is substantial because society is full of messages of who does or doesn't deserve love, and who is and isn't responsible for the bulk of the loving.

Being ambiguous about who might be answering our well-wishes invites the whole interdependent Universe to participate in making our wishes come true. Why control who is responsible for the manifestation of loving-kindness, when there would be so much more loving-kindness if it could spread freely from act to act and from person to person, way beyond the bounds of our imagination?

Let loving-kindness be. Don't try to own it or control it. It doesn't belong to any one of us, and it's one of the few things I would love to see grow profusely out of control everywhere!

2) Changing "may my beloved BE safe..." to "may my beloved FEEL safe..."

I was taken aback when I caught myself doing this one day. I may have been more stressed than usual, but I hadn't noticed that I wasn't feeling safe/healthy/happy/at ease, and yet there I was wishing to feel differently.

It may happen to you.

I decided to pause my practice, and pay attention. What memories, what fears, what sensations, what hopes were surfacing as I wished to feel safe, healthy, happy, and at ease?

And I offered myself a hug.

And then returned to my practice, taking time to offer myself loving-kindness until the tears came.

If you catch yourself unconsciously changing the words in the practice, pause to understand what is revealing itself, and offer yourself the compassion you need. Tears are not required; just your attention.

In any given moment, you may not have the capacity to feel safe, healthy, happy or at ease, even if you know you are safe, healthy, happy or at ease. And sometimes you will know that you are not safe, healthy, happy or at ease, no matter how you feel.

Loving-kindness is a deep desire for safety, health, happiness, and ease in this world for yourself and others. You can experience this desire whether you feel or are safe, healthy, happy and at ease.

Don't settle for the feeling. Ask for the real thing.

Can I change the sequence?

Thanks again for asking! Again, please wait. The language of loving-kindness practice varies by culture and lineage of practice, but the sequence rarely does.

This form has evolved over two thousand five hundred years. There may be wisdom in the details of the practice as it's been transmitted to us. Further evolution may be warranted, but be careful about introducing mutations. We may not fully understand the implications until much later.

Simple is powerful.

There is a progression in "difficulty to wrap your mind around" from safety, to health, to happiness, to ease in the world.

There is a progression in proximity from self, to known others, to unknown others, to the entire Universe.

This second progression rarely coincides with the progression from easier to harder to love. And there's the challenge for most of us. The people closest to us are often both the easiest and hardest to love.

But the progression in proximity is also a progression in accountability. The more deeply woven the relationship, the more impactful our actions.

If it feels selfish or uncomfortable to start with yourself, then consider the possibility that it is irresponsible not to start with yourself. If loving-kindness is a possibility for you, then offer it to yourself first, so that it can nourish your every cell and action. You are not responsible for other people's actions, just yours.

And if it terrifies you to start with yourself, consider the possibility that you have suffered abuse of some kind. Maybe someone taught you something and called it "love" or "kindness" when it was actually harmful. Maybe an adult who was accountable for your well-being as a child intentionally or unintentionally neglected you or hurt you. If so, you need loving-kindness.

Allow yourself to wish yourself safety, health, happiness, and ease in this world, over and over gain, perhaps for a whole practice session or two or three if that is what you need.

Once there is space in your heart for yourself, there will be space in your heart for others. There will be space in your heart for loving-kindness.

Is practicing alone enough?

Yes, of course! Yay for practicing!

And, a community of practice offers support, connection, reality checks, and friends.

Loving-kindness practice is typically just one of many practices of a meditating community. It may not even be in the repertoire of communities of practice around you. Enjoy the variety, and explore what you want to incorporate into your daily meditation practice.

You may already belong to one or more religious, spiritual, or cultural communities. If so, you may want to seek out people within your communities who would like to explore loving-kindness and other forms of meditation with you. Your communities may have their own contemplative traditions and practices that you want to explore. If your community is hostile to wishing for the safety, health, happiness and ease in this world for all people without exception, that may be an indication that loving-kindness practice would be particularly transformative for you.

No matter how you seek or create a community of practice for yourself, honor the integrity of each tradition and practice. Spiritual practices evolve in specific contexts with specific cultural assumptions. Change the context and change the assumptions, and you change the content.

Spiritual practices are also often designed to be challenging. If something seems silly, uncomfortable, unnecessary, or impossible, tap into your compassion and ask why others might find value in it.

Sometimes, joining (or leaving) a community can threaten your safety, health, happiness, and ease in this world. Sometimes not joining (or remaining) is an even greater threat. It's a blessing when we feel that we have a choice.

Finding people that share our values, interests, and commitments is a great joy.

May you that joy be yours!

What next?

I hope you find loving-kindness meditation simple and rewarding. And there is much more to explore beyond what I can offer in this tiny guide.

Here are some ways to deepen and or broaden your meditation practice.

Connect with a community of practice.

If there are meditation groups near you, give them a try. People are always a challenge, and our relationships with people are good barometers of how meditation is affecting how we are in the world.

Learn from authoritative teachers.

Many people have practiced loving-kindness meditation for a long time with other people who have practiced loving-kindness meditation for a long time.

I recommend starting with the work of Sharon Salzberg, the author of the book *Lovingkindness: The Revolutionary Art of Happiness*, and the main source of the specific wording of the practice in this book. She is a teacher in Insight Meditation, a Vipassana Buddhist community.

Pema Chödrön, a nun in the Tibetan Buddhist Vajrayana lineage, offers a loving-kindness practice with the same essence but with very different word choices. Her most recent book that directly addresses loving-kindness is *The Wisdom of No Escape: And the Path of Loving Kindness*.

Try other meditation practices.

If you aren't ready to delve deeper into loving-kindness practice and its Buddhist origins, go for variety and breadth. *Secular Meditation: 32 Practices for Cultivating Inner Peace, Compassion, and Joy A Guide from the Humanist Community at Harvard* by Rick Heller and Greg Epstein may serve you well. The book leans toward a fundamentalist atheism, but it does have a heart for humanity and samples a wide range of meditation practices quite well. It's a great starting point for experimentation.

Invest in tools that would remove obstacles and add joy to your practice.

If you are practicing every day, your practice warrants a few specialized tools.

A comfortable "seat"

I love my meditation cushion. It's soft and sturdy and aqua with green and pink flowers on it! It's always ready for me to plop onto it and begin meditating. With a few wiggles now and then, I am content.

Think of how you want to support yourself physically, and gather the props you need to make that happen. It doesn't need to be something specifically marketed for meditation, but those may work too. Ask other practitioners who share your physical needs for recommendations.

A Timer

Letting someone or something other than yourself keep track of time will help you relax into your practice. Ideally, with minimal action on your part, your timer can give you a gentle reminder of when to start, when to adjust your body or enter a different phase in your practice, and when you're done.

Here are four ideas:

- **A strand of beads** This is a traditional meditation tool in many cultures. Move beads through your fingers one at a time as you take a breath or recite a phrase. You can have different types of beads in your strand to signal different intervals.

- **An hour glass** These may be hard to find, but you can make one yourself. At each transition, you just flip it over. You may also want something like beads to help you keep track of how many times you flipped it.

- **A clock with a dial-face** You can mark intervals with something removable like stickers so you don't have to remember them. I find most clock alarms too jarring during meditation, but you could use an alarm arm as a visual reminder of your end time without setting the alarm to sound. If your concern is falling asleep, then the promise of a nice loud ring may be what helps you relax into your practice.

- **A Smart-Phone App** If you want to go high-tech, I recommend the app *InsightTimer*. The app offers several bell sounds that can be set to sound at customizable intervals. You can also explore guided meditations, yoga practices, and talks from many teachers. Most require a paid subscription plan but many do not. Just remember, you don't know what you're getting in a guided meditation until you try it, so proceed with caution.

Keep paying attention to what matters to you most.

There are people, creatures, beings, stories, issues, advertisements, sounds, sensations, images, emotions, memories, values and world views that continuously clamor for attention. There are those that are just as worthy that get lost in the noise.

It really is difficult to stay focused on what matters most. Meditation can help.

If love, kindness, loving-kindness, people, the beautiful and broken world we share, and our collective well-being matter, loving-kindness meditation can help,

What we pay attention to fills our lives.

What matters most to you? Whatever it is, may it stay close to the center of your attention, and may it fill your life.

Epilogue: How My Life Has Changed Since Starting the Practice

Some say that when people really change, they don't notice it themselves.

Practicing loving-kindness may be effort-full, but the changes that it brings may be effort-less. Or perhaps what used to take a lot of effort, now takes little. Maybe it's because you will still be you, and the world will still be the world, just subtly different, like wearing your hair up in a bun or draped over your shoulders, if you happened to have long hair.

One change I've noticed is that my kitchen counters are more likely to be clear. It used to be that by the end of the day, I resented "having to clean the kitchen." It was another task at the end of a long day of getting things done, and a little voice would say "I don't have to do this now!" The little voice was technically correct, and I would let messes grow until there was no counter space left or the discomfort of living in a smelly clutter grew larger than the discomfort of cleaning up.

The resistance to cleaning is still with me. It's just easier to get the dishes done. My typical morning routine has shifted from waking up and doing the dishes to waking up, brewing a pot of tea, and watching the sun rise.

The other change is that my beloved spouse now shares ten minute "quiet time" with me. I asked him, he said "ok," and now we simply expect that in the morning, before going to work, there will be quiet time. We've been together for almost twenty years, and I don't think either of us imagined that he would say yes to doing anything that could be labelled "spiritual" without a sense of sacrifice. It probably helps that there is increasing clinical evidence for the benefits of meditation.

He enjoys it. Now, he's often the one inviting me to quiet time. Still, I haven't asked him to try loving-kindness practice yet.

Perhaps this tiny guide will change that.

Thank You!

- All the teachers who have kept this practice alive and well
- You, my reader, who honor me with your attention
- Lindsey and Alex who created the opportunity for me to write a Tiny Book!
- Laurel who enthusiastically connects people with people
- Cathey who offered to reign me in from going too rogue
- Sophie who said yes!
- The communities of practice who guide and challenge me
- Eric who took over responsibility for you know what at the moment of you-know-when, creating space in my life to write this book
- Paul who suggested that there is a time to become an elder, and share what we learned
- Eden who inspired me by example
- Yumiko who challenges me to reflect deeply on happiness
- Honor who gave me the English language
- Hisato who cried with me

- Friends and colleagues who explore the overgrown paths of embodied love
- All who have supported me with loving and kind gestures along the way, noticed and unnoticed by be, known and unknown by them
- Mike who effortfully and effortlessly loves me with (almost) every breath

Mahalo and aloha,

Love,

C

About the Author

Catherine's earliest memory of practicing meditation dates back to when she was twelve. Since then, she has begun a meditation practice many times.

Her genetic ancestors come from all over Eurasia, and the most recent among them bequeathed to her Christian, Buddhist, Shinto, Confucian, Humanist, Japanese, and North American White-Anglo-Super-Protestant cultural inheritances that shape her understanding of meditation. Her spiritual ancestors come from all over planet Earth, and increasingly come from Hawai'i, her current home.

She has trained and worked as an astrophysicist and as a minister in the Unitarian Universalist movement, a multi-religious humanistic faith tradition. Her current motto is "Just Love."

Most importantly, Catherine likes belly rubs, shoulder massages, and back scratches.

You can connect with her at `thistoois.com`.

About the Illustrator

Sophie Northcott is a graphic designer and lifeguard in Santa Cruz, California. She can bake cookies and fix your car.

www.ingramcontent.com/pod-product-compliance
Lightning Source LLC
Chambersburg PA
CBHW020913080526
44589CB00011B/570